Introduction to Programming
with Pascal

Lecture Notes

Introduction to Programming with Pascal
Lecture Notes

Paul Gent BSc

Table of Contents

Reading this Book

This Book displays code examples, many of which have long lines. These longer lines should not be broken or wrap over multiple lines like normal text. While every effort has been made to ensure correct formatting, the wide range of font and screen sizes means that some lines may not appear precisely as envisioned by the author.

It is recommended that you read this book to maximize the width of the text display when viewing the code examples. You may also find it useful to reduce the text size to view the code examples as they are meant to be displayed.

Introduction

This book provides a basic introduction to the computer programming using the Pascal programming language. This introduction is designed for programmers and non-programmers alike, and as such it introduces the basic concepts of programming, in general.

This book covers introductory Pascal programming language material, including programs, procedures, common language operators and variables, etc. The material herein focuses on procedural code and does not go into object-oriented programming, although the Pascal language does support these constructs. The Pascal language is used in a number of free and commercial programming tools. An excellent free Pascal tool is called Lazarus.

Write and Writeln - Simple Output

The write and writeln commands output text to the screen or the standard output device:

```
write ('#')
```

Outputs a # character to the screen.
Single quote marks are used in Pascal to surround a string or character to denote it as such.

```
write (23)
```

Outputs the number 23 to the screen.

```
write (20, '/', 8, '/', 2019)
```

Outputs the given text (which is a date) like so: 20/8/2019
Multiple items (strings, characters, contents of variables, numerical data) can be printed like this from within a single write or writeln command.

```
write ('Hello')
```

Outputs the *string* Hello

```
writeln ('Enter a number: ')
```

Outputs the string inside the single quotes and then moves the cursor to the start of the next line on the screen.

```
writeln
```

Causes the output to go to the start of the next line on screen.

Statements

Lines of code (commands) are called statements in Pascal. Statements are *executed*, i.e. carried out when the program is run.

Statements are ended or separated by a semicolon **;**

Sample code:

```
writeln('Hello Dave');
writeln;
write('I am fine.');
```

Produces the following output:

```
Hello Dave

I am fine.
```

The first line prints the text *Hello Dave* exactly as it appears inside the single quotes, then moves the cursor to the start of the next line. The second line of code again moves the cursor to the start of the next line causing a blank line to be output. The third line of code prints the text *I am fine.* and leaves the cursor at the end of the line after the period or full stop.

Note the *semicolon* at the end of each line and the use of *single quotes* to surround the text.

A Simple Complete Program

```
program helloworld;
begin
   write('Hello ');
   writeln('World!');
end.
```

The output from this program is:

```
Hello World!
```

helloworld is the name of the program – you can use any valid name to name your programs. Valid variable naming is discussed later in the book.

A program is surrounded by a *begin* and an *end* statement (like the curly braces in C or C++ if you are familiar with that language) to mark the start and finish of the program.

A program ends with an *end.* (end then a period or full stop).

Indentation of Statements

Statements (code) are indented to make logical sections easier to read by a human. Indentation in Pascal has no bearing on the computer (it does in a few other languages) however it is good practice to indent code so that you and other programmers can read it easily and so that you can follow the flow of the code. In professional environments, there are standards used for indentation of statements and for naming of variables etc. You should follow the standards laid out for you, or follow those already existing in code if you are collaborating with a team.

In these notes I use a simple indentation layout to help the learning process, and use two spaces as the default indent. This makes it easy to read on any operating system and in printed code.

Many programming editors will automatically indent code for you so that it is easier to read.

Comments

Comments in code are used to explain the statements or provide human readable notes and information. Comments are not read by the compiler and are ignored by the computer. They are only there to help or inform the programmer.

Comments and comment blocks in a program are enclosed in curly brackets / braces **{ }**. Single lines comments can be created by using two forward slashes **//**.

A comment can exist on a line on its own, or on a line that also contains code.

To End Of Line Comment

```
writeln('2015'); // assume this year
```

The above shows a statement with a comment on the same line. The two slashes comment means that everything AFTER the two slashes, until the end of the current line, is considered a comment and ignored by the compiler.

Note: This comment style may not exist for all Pascal based compilers / integrated development environments (IDEs).

Single Line, In Code and Multi-Line Comments

```
writeln ('Hello World!'); {displays the text}
```

The above is a comment at the end of a line using the curly brackets. Likewise because these comments have a begin and an end, and do not rely on the end of line like the two slashes comment, you can insert a comment in the middle of a statement.

```
writeln {displays the text} ('Hello World!');
```

The comment is ignored even though it is in the middle of the statement.

```
{Printing out the Hello World!
Text so it appears on a single line}
write ('Hello');
writeln (' World! ');
```

The above comment is over two lines. Everything from the opening curly bracket to the closing curly bracket is considered a comment. Comments can be many lines if needed.

Remember to close your comments if you are using block or multi-line comments. Most programming editors will highlight comments in a different color to make them easier to see and to show where they begin and end.

Reserved Words

Reserved words are key words that are predefined and used in Pascal as part of the language and cannot be reused as variable names.

Examples of reserved words include:

program – Denotes the start of a program.
begin – Denotes the start of a code block, will have a corresponding end.
end – Denotes the end of a code block, will have a corresponding begin.
var – Denotes that a variable declaration is coming.
const – Denotes that a constant declaration is coming.
for, *repeat* and *while* – Are all reserved words used with loops

You will see examples of these and additional reserved words as you continue.

Identifiers

An identifier is a name for things in Pascal. Identifiers include the names for procedures, function, programs, variable, etc.

Identifier names follow the same rules as for variable names which are described in the next section.

Variables

A variable is a container that holds a value that the program will work on. It is a little piece of storage space in the memory used by the program that holds a value that can be changed. Variables can hold many different types of values like numbers, characters, and text.

A variable must be declared in a program before it is used by the program, so the program knows what type of data it will hold and how much memory the variable could occupy so that it can allocate space for it and knows how to use it.

When declaring a variable, the *type* of the variable i.e. the type of data it will hold, must be specified. Whole numbers are referred to as *integer*. Numbers with a decimal point in them (floating point numbers) are referred to as *real*.

A single character like the letter A, is referred to as a *char*. Strings or text which is made up of multiple characters is referred to as a *string*.

When a variable is first declared in a program it holds no valid value. You have to assign a starting or initial value before you can rely on what the variable holds.

Variable Naming Rules

Variables in Pascal can have any name, as long as they follow the rules outlined below.

- Variable names must **start with a letter** and **contain only letters, numbers and the underscore character** _.

- Variable names can be as long as you like (up to 127 characters) and must not contain spaces.

Pascal as a language is case-insensitive, i.e. uppercase letters are considered the same as lowercase letters, hence varying case makes no difference to a Pascal program (case does matter for other languages!).

For example:

FirstName is same variable name as *firstname* or *firSTNAMe*, **LINE1** is the same variable name as **line1** and so on.

Note that the program name is also a variable and hence follows the naming rules.

Any variable name must not be the same as a reserved word of Pascal (e.g. begin, end, program, procedure, integer etc.)

Sample Complete Program

```pascal
program findbiggest;
var
  num1, num2 : integer;
begin
  write ('Enter number 1: ');
  readln (num1);
  write ('Enter number 2: ');
  readln (num2);

  if (num1 > num2) then
    writeln('The first number is Larger.');
  else
  begin
    if (num2 > num1) then
      writeln('The second number is Larger.')
    else
      writeln('The numbers are Equal.')
  end;
end.
```

Sample Program Explanation

The sample program declares and uses two variables. These are called *num1* and *num2*. These variables are declared to store values of type *integer*. Each variable can hold a single value. When these variables are created they do not have any value stored in them and you should not assume they are set to any initial value as one has not been specified.

The program then displays a message to the user asking for entry of a number, and accepting that entry and storing the value into num1. This process is repeated for num2.

The *readln* command allows you to accept user input, in this case from the keyboard, and after the user has enters the input it moves the cursor to the next line. There is also a corresponding *read* command which does not move the cursor to the next line.

The program then compares num1 and num2 to evaluate which holds the biggest value or if they are equal, printing a message stating the findings before ending. The reserved word *if* is used to test a Boolean expression, an if is followed by the test it is to evaluate and finally a *then* reserved word after that. An if statement evaluates to either True or False, and can include multiple tests together to result in a single true or false result. The code statement or block following the *then* reserved word is executed when the evaluation results in a true value.

The optional *else* reserved word is used for the code to be executed when the if evaluates to false. The else portion is optional and not required, but can be useful to allow you to branch code for the two possibilities (what to do when the test is either true or false).

Because the else portion of the if statement has multiple statements it is surrounded by a begin and an end to create a block of code. Multiple lines of code can be included inside a block of code. Good indentation is important so the code is easily readable and it is clear what lines of code are included inside a block or outside a block. Remember indentation does not affect the code, it is only to make it easier to read.

When the program ends, the memory used for the program including the variables declared at the start of the program is released back to the operating system.

Exercise: Write a program similar to the above that adds two numbers entered by the user and prints if the sum is greater than 100.

Assigning Values to Variables

An assignment statement is used to put a value into a variable. The assignment characters are := (colon then equals sign).

For example, you declare a variable called StreetNum and want to put the value of 300 in it:

```
var
   StreetNum : Integer;
begin
   StreetNum := 300;
```

You can also use expressions (calculations) on the right had side of the assignment statement. In these cases the value of the expression is determined and the resulting value placed in the variable:

```
StreetNum := 300 + 20;
// StreetNum is now holding a value
// of 320
```

or

```
StreetNum := StreetNum + 1;
// Adds 1 to the current value
// in StreetNum
```

Expressions can also contain variables, function calls (more on that later) and complex math.

```
StreetNum := ((300 - OldStreetNum) * 2) - 1;
// The value to the right of the :=
// is calculated first
```

Be careful not to use the = (equals) sign alone. An = sign means test for equality, not assign a value to.

If statement

The *if* statement allows you to test if an expression is *true* or *false*, and then act on the result.

For example:

```
if (num > 100) then
   writeln('Number is greater than 100')
else
   writeln('Number is less than or equal to 100');
```

The condition, *num > 100*, is evaluated and if it evaluates to *true*, the code or code block after the *then* reserved word is executed. Any code after the optional *else* reserved word is skipped.

However, if the condition evaluates to *false*, the code or code block after the *else* reserved word is executed and the code after the *then* reserved word is skipped. Note: The else section is optional, you can have an if without an else.

As for other code blocks if you use the reserved words begin and end, you can have multiple lines of code in an if statement.

```
if (num > 100) then
begin
   write('Number is greater than 100');
   writeln;
end
else
begin
   write('Number is less than or equal to 100');
   writeln:
end;
```

Examining the code, note that you should not have a semicolon ; before an else, either on a single line of code, or after the end for a block of code.

Multiple if statements

Multiple if statements can be combined to give more than two possible outcomes:

```
if (num > 0) then
   writeln('Number is greater than 0')
else
begin
   if (num = 0) then
      writeln('Number is equal to 0');
   else
      writeln('Number is less than 0');
end;
```

Notice the use of the begin and end block to create a block for the second if statement. If you do not use a begin and end block you need to remember that any else statement will work with the nearest if, and indentation of code does not matter.

Remember that when working with multiple if statements, always use the begin and end reserved words to create clear code blocks so that you do not make errors in the logic of your expression and so that the code is readable.

Constants

Constants are values that have a name. They are named in the same way and according to the same rules as variables but the value in a constant cannot be changed. The value can only be assigned to the constant once when it is first declared. The reserved word *const* is used to denote a constant.

An example of a real world constant is the value for Pi, which is 3.1.415... The value for Pi does not change.

To define a const in your code, simply say:

```
const
   pi = 3.141592653;
```

The const pi can now be used in your code rather than typing out all the digits in the number each time.

In the below sample program you can see the definition of a const called x and its use in the main code.

```
program consts;
const
   x = 4;
var
   a : integer;
begin
   write('Enter a number: ');
   readln(a);
   writeln(a, ' + ', x, ' = ', a+x);
end.
```

Program Output:

```
Enter a number: 5
5 + 4 = 9
```

Operators

+ is the Pascal symbol for addition

- is the Pascal symbol for subtraction

* is the Pascal symbol for multiplication

/ is the Pascal symbol for division

( ) Brackets can be used in expressions as you would normally expect in mathematics. Nested brackets are also permitted. Brackets can also be used for clarity to make it easier to read complex calculations and expressions.

= is the test for equality (equals)

< > is the test for inequality (not equals) – This is a left angle bracket < followed by a right angled bracket >

Loops

Loops are essential tools in programming as they allow controlled repetition of code. There are a number of different types of loops and we will look at the most commonly used.

For Loop

A *for* loop allows you to repeat a block of code a finite number of times, as well as optionally allowing you to break out of the loop early, if desired.

```
program sum5;
var
   numtotal, num, x : integer;
begin
   { Initialize the running total
     variable to hold 0 }
   numtotal:= 0;

   // Loop 5 times
   for x:= 1 to 5 do
   begin
      write('Enter number ',x ,' : ');
      // Read in number
      readln(num);
      // Add number to running total
      numtotal:= numtotal + num;
   end;   // end for loop
   writeln('The Sum is ',numtotal)
end.
```

Note the use of multiple parameters in the call to write in this program, this allows you to have multiple sections in your write call which helps keep your code easy to read and allows you to build up the text to display in a single call.

The previous program uses a *for* loop to read in five numbers, specified by the control value in the for loop, which counts from *1 to 5* automatically incrementing by 1 each time. The control value is stored in the *control variable* which is defined as *x* in the program.

The five numbers are read in to a variable *num*, once each time around the loop. Then the value help in the variable *num* as added to the running total which is the *numtotal* variable.

The for loop runs from the *begin* which appears directly after the for loop statement and ends at the *end;* statement. The end line includes the comment *// end for loop* to show its logical use and which block of code it applies to. The indentation used should also help show the contents of the for loop.

After the loop has completed its five iterations, the value in the *numtotal* variable is written out to provide the running total for the numbers entered.

The control variable in the for loop which is called x could be called anything else according to the variable naming rules, and is automatically incremented by 1 each time around the loop. The control variable starts at the starting value (1) and ends at the ending value (5) resulting in 5 iterations of the loop.

You should not manually modify the value of the for loop control variable in your own code. If you need to leave the loop early you can use the reserved word *break* to break out of the loop and go to the next line of code after the end of the for loop. Likewise you should not reuse the same control variable twice in nested for loops (loops inside loops) as the inner loop changes to the control variable would modify the outer loops control variable value. In these cases you should declare additional variables to act as the control variable for second and subsequent nested loops.

The for loop starting and ending values can be expressions and in this case should be surrounded by brackets:

```
for count:= 14 to (numlines - 1) do
```

In addition to integers as the control loop type, other ordinal values can also be used. For example, you could use characters char as the control variable and count from a to z, as their ASCII values allow us to increment by one and progress from a to b to c, and so on to z.

```
program printalphabet;
var
   letter : char;
begin
   for letter:= a to z do
     write(letter);
end.
```

Will write out all the letters of the alphabet from a to z without any spaces between each letter.

Note in the *for* loop used here there is no begin or end statement around the block of code. This is because there is only a single statement (line of code) so the compiler knows that that single line "belongs" to the for loop. More on blocks of statements later.

While Loop

A *while* loop allows you to repeat a block of code while some criteria is met e.g. until a test to stay the loop becomes false. You can optionally break out of the loop early, if desired.

Here is an example of a while loop that adds all the numbers entered and continues until the number entered by the user is 0:

```
sum := 0;
readln(num);
while (num <> 0) do
  begin
    sum := sum + num;
    readln(num)
  end;
```

The syntax of a while loop is:
> **while** *condition* **do** *statement(s)*

This means that while the *condition* is evaluated to be *true* then the *statement(s)* is performed. When the *condition* evaluates as *false* the loop ends and the line of code after the end of the while loop is executed.

The statement(s) can be one or more lines of code. If it is multiple lines of code it should be surrounded by a begin and end block.

The example can be enhanced to exit if a 0 or a -1 is entered:

```
program addup;
var
  sum, num : integer;
begin
  sum := 0;
  readln(num);
  while ( (num <> 0) and (num <> -1) ) do
  begin
    sum := sum + num;
    readln(num)
  end;
  writeln('Sum of numbers entered = ',sum);
end.
```

Notice the use of brackets to make the condition part of the while loop evaluate correctly, while the first expression num <> 0 and the second expression num <> -1 are both true the loop will continue, but once one of the expressions evaluates to false the loop will end.

In a while loop the condition controlling the while loop is only evaluated between iterations of the loop statement and not continuously. This means that the value of num could be 0 at some point during the statements (if there were more statements than what is shown in the example) but the loop will only exit if num is 0 or -1 when the test for the condition is evaluated which is the first time the loop is started and then after the last line of the statements in the loop.

Given this condition evaluation at the start of the first loop, it is possible the loop will not start if the condition fails, in which case the value displayed will be 0 as no numbers have been entered.

Repeat Loop

A *repeat* loop is similar to a while loop except that the evaluation is at the end of the loop after the reserved word *until*, so the repeat loop will always occur at least once, and the evaluation is to test when to stop the loop rather than the while loop which is a test to start the loop.

```
sum := 0;
repeat
   readln(num);
   sum := sum + num;
until (num = 0);
```

The syntax of a repeat loop is:
> **repeat** *statement(s)* **until** *condition*

The repeat loop does not require a begin and end block around the statements no matter how many statements there are.

```
program addup_repeat;
var
   sum, num : integer;
begin
   sum := 0;
   readln(num);
   repeat
      sum := sum + num;
      readln(num)
   until ( (num = 0) or (num = -1) );
   writeln('Sum of numbers entered = ',sum);
end.
```

Procedures

A *procedure* is a name given to a block of code that can be executed by calling the name of the procedure. It is commonly used to allow code reuse and to logically separate code for readability and testing purposes. A procedure can be called any number of times from a main program or from other procedures, allowing reuse of code.

A procedure often looks like a mini-program can contain all of the elements of a program such as variables and statements. There is no limit to the size of a procedure nor the number of variables and statements it can contain.

The following program outputs a right angled triangle of stars. The program contains a procedure which prints a number of stars when it is called. The procedure accepts an integer value so it knows how many stars to output. The procedure is called *stars*. The program asks the user for the size of the triangle and then outputs that triangle uses for loops.

```
program print_stars;

   procedure stars (num_stars: integer);
   var
      i : integer;
   begin
      for i := 1 to num_stars do
         write('*');
      writeln;
   end;

var
   tri_size, x : integer;

begin
   write('Triangle size: ');
   readln(tri_size);
   for x := 1 to tri_size do
      stars(x);
end.
```

The output from this program looks like this:

```
Triangle size: 7
*
**
***
****
*****
******
*******
```

Code explanation:

The program starts with the standard program reserved word and identifier for the program.

It then includes the declaration for a procedure called *stars*. This procedure accepts an integer value as a parameter called *num_stars*. num_stars in this example is a variable of type integer for use only in the procedure. The procedure also includes a variable *i* of type integer which will be the control variable for the for loop in the main code of the procedure.

The main program (underneath the procedure code) includes two integer variables, and some statements to read in a value from the keyboard and store that value in the variable *tri_size*.

The procedure is *called* in the main program by using its name along with any parameters required in brackets after the name. The parameters entered when calling a procedure will match the order and type of the parameters declared in the declaration of the procedure. In this case there is only a single parameter of type integer.

When the procedure is called, it copies the parameter value passed in from the main program (which is stored in the variable *tri_size*) into *num_stars*. The procedure then executes its statements and uses num_stars to determine the size of the for loop.

When the procedure is finished, execution returns to the main program and the line after the call to the procedure is executed next.

It is important to understand the difference between declaring a procedure and calling it in code:

A Procedure Declaration defines what the procedure should do.

A Procedure Call is a statement itself and it commands the procedure to be executed.

In general a procedure has the following components:

A Procedure Declaration starts with the word *procedure* followed by the name of the procedure (which must follow the rules for variable naming, see later in this book).

After the name of the procedure comes the optional parameters inside brackets and then a semicolon;

Then any local variables are declared, followed by a begin statement, then the code for the procedure ending with an end, and lastly a semicolon.

Procedures can contain additional procedures inside them and these are called *nested procedures*.

Variables declared within a procedure are referred to as *local* variables to that procedure and cannot be accessed outside of the procedure. These local variables only exist inside the procedure and while the procedure is executing.

Exercise: Write a program using a simple procedure to read in any five numbers the user enters and displays the average of the entered numbers.

Possible Solution (there are many ways to solve this exercise):

```
program sum5;

  procedure sum_nums;
  var
    i, user_num, sum : integer;
  begin
    sum := 0;
    for i := 1 to 5 do
    begin
      write('   Enter number ', i, ': ');
      readln(user_num);
      sum := sum + user_num;
    end;
    writeln('The sum is: ', sum);
  end;

begin
  writeln('This program will add any 5 integers.');
  writeln('Please enter the 5 integers:');
  sum_nums;
end.
```

Output from the Program:

```
This program will add any 5 integers.
Please enter the 5 integers:
   Enter number 1: 2
   Enter number 2: 5
   Enter number 3: 8
   Enter number 4: 4
   Enter number 5: 3
The sum is: 22
```

Procedures Continued

It is good programming practice to write self contained code, e.g. procedures and this style of programming allows for easy reuse of code and makes code easier to read.

> *Declare Before Use* rule – Variables and code entities (such as procedures) can only be referred to, after they have been declared, this is known as scope and is discussed a little later.

One procedure can call another procedure and in general, the *Declare Before Use* rule applies to procedures, so procedure B can call procedure A, but only if procedure A is declared above procedure B.

But what happens if procedure A needs to be able to call procedure B, and procedure B needs to be able to call procedure A?

Procedure Prototyping

Procedure Prototyping is a way to state that the code for the Procedure will come later but allows you to call or reference the Procedure from a point in the code above or before the code. It is also known as *forward declaration* and uses the reserved word **forward** to indicate this in code.

```
program procs;

  procedure Alpha (a : integer); Forward;

  procedure Beta (b : integer);
  begin
    Alpha(b);
  end;

  procedure Alpha (a : integer);
  begin
   writeln(a + 2);
  end;

begin
  Beta(5);
end.
```

In this example, the Procedure Alpha uses the *Forward* reserved word to tell the compiler that the code for the procedure will come later. This forward declaration includes the minimum information about the procedure, namely what it is called and what parameters it accepts. What code is in the procedure is not going to be defined until later, but this is OK as any calls to the procedure Alpha can now be validated to be correct against the procedure declaration, i.e. any calls to Alpha must use the correct name and the correct parameters, regardless of what the procedure will do.

Later in the code the full definition of the procedure is stated. If you omit the full definition you will receive an error during compilation of your code like *Unsatisfied Forward* or *Forward Declaration Missing*.

Parameters in Procedures

Procedures can include parameters which accept a value.

```
procedure printnumplusone (num: integer);
begin
   num:=num+1;
   write(num);
end;
```

There are three basic types of parameter, the standard *formal* parameter you have seen already, and the *var* and *const* parameters. There are other types of parameter but for now we will only review the basic types.

The *formal* parameter allows you to pass a value into a procedure and use it or change it within the procedure. Any changes to the value of the parameter are lost when the procedure ends and this value is not passed back to where it was called from.

As discussed earlier, a *var* is a variable in that its value can be changed, but a *const* cannot have its value changed once it is initially set. These definitions also apply to parameters.

In the printnum procedure below the value in num is set each time the procedure is called and cannot be changed for that call of the procedure. The code below uses num but does not and cannot change it. Note the difference in usage, num can never change during the life of the procedure as it is defined as a *const*.

```
procedure printnum (const num: integer);
begin
   write(num);
end;
```

Formal and var parameters, and the values or variables these parameters are called with must be of the same type (or compatible).

For example, calling printnumplusone with a string rather than the required integer would result in an error.

If you need to be able to change the value passed into the procedure and retain that value after the procedure has completed executing its code, you can set the parameter to be *var*. This indicates that any changes to the parameter will be passed back to where it was called from, and this also introduces a new rule for calling procedures with var parameters, you cannot call them with a value, you must call them with another variable so there is somewhere to store the value that is passed back.

```
procedure getnumplusone (var num: integer);
begin
   num:=num+1;
end;
```

An example of calling getnumplusone would look like:

```
var
   y : integer;
begin
   y := 1;
   getnumplusone(y);
   writeln(y);
```

As demonstrated the value of num is changed by the procedure so it must have a variable to store the changed value in, when it is passed back to where it is called from. In this case y starts out as 1 and it gets passed into getnumplusone via the var parameter num. num is changed to 2 in the procedure, then the value of 2 is passed back to y.

When y is written out, it will display 2 as this is the value that has been passed back to it.

Exercise: Write a program containing a procedure that uses a var parameter and changes the value of the parameter in the program.

Functions

Functions look and act similarly to Procedures, except they add the ability to directly return a value. In this sense a function call is an expression, i.e. it calculates something and *returns* a value. A function can have many lines of code just like a procedure.

An example of a function is one that returns the average of three numbers:

```
function avg3 (const x, y, z :real) : real;
begin
   result := ( x + y + z ) / 3;
end;
```

This function is called avg3, and accepts 3 constant real values (values with a decimal point in them) and at the end of the function will also return a real value. All functions must specify a return type, this is the type of value the function will provide when it is called. This is done by have a : after the parameters, and the type after the colon.

The function uses the reserved word *result* to specify what value to send back to the function call.

An example of calling this function in a program looks like:

```
program test3;

   function avg3 (const x, y, z :real) : real;
   begin
      result := ( x + y + z ) / 3;
   end;

var
   n : real;
begin
   n := avg3(1.1, 2.4, 5.67);
   writeln('The average is ', n);
   ...
```

In the above example, n is a variable of type real, and is uninitialized, in that it has no defined starting value. The function avg3 is called with 3 values, 1.1, 2.4 and 5.67. The function calculates the average value and passes back or *returns* the calculated value to the calling program, in this case the variable n is assigned the value that the function returns. n now holds the average of the three numbers and can be used going forward.

In general, the goal of a function is to be a self contained piece of code and be independent so they can be called with only their parameters required. As such functions should not use var parameters as they value they pass back should be handled with the result reserved word for the specified return type, however it is possible to use var parameters should they be required.

Note: It is permissible to use the function name in place of the *result* reserved word, however I recommend you use result for code clarity, at least in the early stages of your programming with Pascal.

Exercise: Write a program that calls the above function after reading the values to be passed into the function from the keyboard, and then have the program display the average.

Write and Writeln – Fieldwidth and Formatting

In the previous example program test3, the writeln displays the following:

```
The average is   3.0566666666666666E+000
```

Which is difficult to read and not user friendly. To allow you to format output such as this, you can use the fieldwidth properties of the write and writeln command.

Fieldwidth is the number of character positions to use for output. It can also optionally control how many character positions are used after the decimal point for numerical data.

For example:

```
write('Pascal', 100:6, 'X':2);
```
is written out as `Pascal    100 X`

To explain, the string 'Pascal' is written out followed by the number 100, which is allocated a fieldwidth of 6 character positions. As the number 100 is 3 character positions, there are 3 blank spaces before it, for a total of 6 character positions. The string 'X' is allocated 2 character positions so there is a blank space before the X.

Fieldwidth is very useful for table and column position formatting. For example review the following loop:

```
for x := 1 to 12 do
   writeln(x:2, x*10:4);
```

Produces the following table:

```
 1   10
 2   20
 3   30
 4   40
 5   50
 6   60
 7   70
 8   80
 9   90
10  100
11  110
12  120
```

There are 2 character positions for the value of x, followed by 4 character positions for the value of x multiplied by 10.

If the fieldwidth specified after the colon is too small it is automatically increased to be just enough to allow the data to be displayed.

`writeln(1000:3)` 3 is not enough character positions, so it automatically increases to the minimum required, which is 4. Care should be taken with this sort of output formatting to ensure data does not touch or it may not be easily readable.

Fieldwidth and the Decimal Point

When you are writing out a number with a decimal point (type real), you may optionally specify both the total fieldwidth and the number of decimal places by using a second colon as shown.

For example:

```
for x := 1 to 3 do
   writeln(x:2, ((x + 10.4)*89):12:3);
```

The fieldwidth of the calculation is a total of 12 character positions, with 3 reserved for after the decimal point. The decimal point also uses one of the 12 character positions in the fieldwidth. The output from this code looks like:

```
1      1014.600
2      1103.600
_3_-_-1192.600
```

On line 3 I have highlighted the blank characters with _ and – to make them visible.

The fieldwidth for x is 2, it therefore has 2 character positions, and the value of x appears right justified in that space. The calculation has a total fieldwidth of 12 character positions, with 3 positions after the decimal point. Counting the characters we see that there are 4 blanks, then 4 digits, then a decimal point, then 3 digits for a total of 12 character positions.

If the optional number of decimal places is omitted, then the output looks like this:

```
for x := 1 to 3 do
   writeln(x:2, ((x + 10.4)*89):12);
```

```
1 1.015E+0003
2 1.104E+0003
3 1.193E+0003
```

Scientific notation can be hard to read, so care should be taken when writing values of type real.

Read and Readln

You have already seen some simple usage of readln to read in numbers from the keyboard, readln and the corresponding read command allow you to read values that are placed into variables from the keyboard, and later on you will see that that can also be used to work with files.

read reads a value from the keyboard and leaves the cursor on the same line just after the value it has read in.

readln performs the same work, but moves the cursor to the start of the next line skipping anything else on the line after the value it has read in.
In general, you will use read only when you have multiple inputs on a single line, which is more common with files than keyboard input.

You can read in many different types using the *readln* command.
Integer – Spaces in input are skipped until an integer value is read in. The numbers in the input must be followed by an <Enter> or a <Space> or else the read will fail.

Real – Similar to Integer and must end with an <Enter> or a <Space>. If a single period (decimal point character) is encountered it is considered part of the number and any digits after the period are the values after the decimal point.

Character – Numbers, letters and punctuation are all considered to be a character. Any single character including an <Enter> or a <Space> will be read as a character.

String – A string is multiple characters, and all input will be read in until an <Enter> is encountered. <Space>, numbers, characters are all part of a string.

Strings

Strings, such as when you enter your name, are actually one-dimensional arrays of characters (an array of type Char).

Generally in Pascal strings are long strings, which can contain a huge number of characters, so they expand and contract dynamically, depending on how many characters you assign to them. You declare long string variables using the reserved word *string*.

Short strings can contain up to a maximum of 255 characters. When you declare a variable of type *shortstring*, you specify the size of the string, much as you specify the size of an array when you declare an array type. Short strings are useful in data structures where you need a fixed-size component.

Depending on the implementation of Pascal you are using the reserved word *string* may actually refer to a short string. You may also want to use *AnsiString* or *WideString*. You will need to look at the documentation of the Pascal compiler or Integrated Development Environment to see what type of string you are using.

These are some string variable declarations:

```
var
  bigstring: string;          {Dynamic size, can hold a huge
                               amount of data}
  myname: string[25];         {Can hold 25 characters}
  littlestring: string[1];    {very short string that only
                               holds a single character}
  string255: shortstring;     {special string type of size 255}
```

These declarations declare the myname variable to contain up to 25 characters and the littlestring variable to contain 1 character. If no size is specified, the string is a long string, as is the case with the bigstring variable.

You can then declare variables of these character arrays just as you would with any other data type.

You can assign a value to a string variable or property by enclosing the sequence of characters that make up the string in single quotation marks ' .

For example:

```
myname := 'Frank P. Matthews';
```

Because myname is a variable of type string[25], which holds 25 characters, myname is stored in memory as if the string were 'Frank P. Matthews '. If you assigned the string 'Frank P. Matthews the Second' to the myname variable, myname would contain the string 'Frank P. Matthews the Secon', because the myname variable can hold only 25 characters.

Pascal short strings are stored as arrays of characters in memory, but the arrays are actually one byte bigger than size of the specified string. The first position of the string, [0], is a byte that contains the size of the string.

Because strings are arrays of characters, you can access characters within a string with an index value, just as you would in an array.

For example:

```
myname[1]
```

refers to the first letter contained in the myname string variable.

Operators

There are a number of operators, some of which differ from other programming languages, and are listed here with brief explanations.

<	Less Than, is the left side less than the right side
<=	Less Than or Equal, is the left side less than or equal to the right side
>	Greater Than, is the left side greater than the right side
>=	Greater Than or Equal, is left side greater than or equal to the right side
=	Equal, is the left side equal to the right side
<>	Not equal, is the left side not equal to the right side (this is a less than sign followed by a greater than sign)

+	Addition
-	Subtraction
*	Multiplication
/	Division e.g. real division which results in a value with a decimal point
div	Integer division, e.g. division resulting in a whole number where any reminder is discarded (see mod)
mod	The remainder left after integer division, e.g. *8 div 3 = 2* and has a remainder of 2, therefore *8 mod 3 = 2*
and	Boolean and, e.g. if (x < 10) and (y < 10) – if both sides of the and is true then the result is true
or	Boolean or, e.g. if (x < 10) or (y < 10) – if either of the two sides of the or is true then the result is true
not	Inverts a Boolean value, e.g. not y results in a true response if y is false, not false = true

Precedence

Operators are applied / evaluated in an order depending on their precedence, with the operators with highest precedence being evaluated first, from left to right.

The order of precedence is provided below:

Highest Precedence is   *not*
Then   ** / div mod and*
Then   *+ - or*
Lowest Precedence   *=*

Example: `10 / 5 * 3 + 2 div 4`

is evaluated in same way as

`( ( (10 / 5) * 3) + (2 div 4) )`

Regardless of the precedence, it is important that you use brackets to make complex expressions readable by others reviewing your code.

Useful built-in functions

Listed here are some useful functions to help you know the names of commonly used functions. You can look up each of these functions in the help or online to see specific examples and usage information but an all in one example is provided below.

Numeric Handling

abs   Absolute value

char   The character which has ASCII value X

ord   The ordinal value of any variable, e.g. the ASCII of a character

round   Rounds a number to the nearest Integer

trunc   Truncates a number dropping anything after the decimal point

mod   The modulus (remainder) after integer division

div   Integer division, discarding any remainder

pred   Returns the predecessor of the ordinal value of a variable without changing the variable (x - 1)

succ   Returns the successor of the ordinal value of a variable without changing the variable (x + 1)

inc   Increments a variable to its successor, variable is changed (x + 1)

dec   Decrements a variable to its predecessor, variable is changed (x - 1)

String Handling

concat   Concatenates multiple strings, creating a larger string. You can also concatenate strings together using the plus sign (+)

copy   Returns a substring within a string

delete   Deletes a specified number of characters from a string beginning at specified position within the string

insert   Inserts another string within a string

length   Returns the length of the string

pos   Returns the position (index) of a substring within a string

All in One Example Program

```pascal
program commonfunctions;
var
  s : string;
  x : integer;
begin
  writeln('abs(-1) = ', abs(-1));
  writeln('char(66) = ', char(66));
  writeln('ord(''A'') = ', ord('A'));
    // Note double single quotes to print a single quote mark on
    // previous line
  writeln('round(2.56) = ', round(2.56));
  writeln('trunc(2.56) = ', trunc(2.56));
  writeln('7 mod 2 = ', 7 mod 2);
  writeln('7 div 2 = ', 7 div 2);
  writeln('pred(8) = ', pred(8));
  writeln('succ(8) = ', succ(8));

  x := 3; writeln('x := 3');
  inc(x);
  writeln('inc(x) = ', x);
  dec(x);
  writeln('dec(x) = ', x);

  writeln('concat(''A'',''B'',''CDE'') = ', concat('A','B','CDE'));
  writeln('copy(''ABCDEFGH'', 2, 3) = ', copy('ABCDEFGH', 2, 3));
  s:='ABCDEFGH';
  delete(s, 2, 3);
  writeln('delete(s, 2, 3) = ', s);
  insert('XYZ', s, 2);
  writeln('insert(''XYZ'', s, 2) = ', s);
  writeln('length(s) = ', length(s));
  writeln('pos(''X'', s) = ', pos('X', s));
end.
```

Output:

`abs(-1) = 1`	*Absolute value of a number*
`char(66) = B`	*The character represented by the ordinal value (ASCII)*
`ord('A') = 65`	*The ordinal (ASCII) value of a character*
`round(2.56) = 3`	*Rounds a number to the nearest integer*
`trunc(2.56) = 2`	*Truncates a number, removing everything after the decimal point*
`7 mod 2 = 1`	*The remainder after Integer division*
`7 div 2 = 3`	*Division where any fractional portion is discarded (Integer Division)*
`pred(8) = 7`	*The Predecessor of the current value*
`succ(8) = 9`	*The Successor of the current value*
`x := 3`	*Assignment to variable x*
`inc(x) = 4`	*Increment the value in variable x by 1*
`dec(x) = 3`	*Decrement the value in variable x by 1*

`concat('A','B','CDE') = ABCDE`	*Concatenate all the strings provided*
`copy('ABCDEFGH', 2, 3) = BCD`	*Copies from the starting position for a specified number of characters*
`delete(s, 2, 3) = AEFGH`	*Deletes from the starting position a specified number of characters*
`insert('XYZ', s, 2) = AXYZEFGH`	*Inserts from the starting position the specified string*
`length(s) = 8`	*Returns the number of characters in the string*
`pos('X', s) = 2`	*Returns the first position of X in the string s*

Case statement

A *case* statement is like an if statement except that in place of true or false, you can define multiple branches as well as an else block.

```
var
   ch: char;
begin
   readln(ch);
   case ch of
      'a', 'e', 'i', 'o', 'u' : writeln('That is a vowel.');
      'y' : writeln('That is the letter Y.');
      'n' : begin
               write('That is the letter ');
               writeln(' N.');
            end
   else
   begin
      writeln('That is not a vowel, nor a Y nor an N.'
   end;
   end;
end.
```

The *case* statement evaluates for each section. A section can have multiple values that can be true, as in the above example where all the vowels are included in a single section.

There is also an optional else section which applies if none of the above sections evaluate to true. In the above example entering the letter h would allow the else section to be executed.

Sections can be single statements, or use a begin and end to create a code block.

Scope

Scope is a definition of where you can call a variable or identifier. Once declared, scope is the code where the declaration is visible and can be called in code. For example, the scope of an identifier declared in a procedure or function declaration stretches from the point of the declaration to the end of the current block, and includes all blocks enclosed by the current block. In other words, variables and types declared within a procedure or function can only be used within that procedure or function.

Identifiers can be redeclared within blocks, this allows for duplicate identifiers within a program, but that identifier can only have a single definition within a block.

For example:

```
program Outer;        { Start of program outer scope }
type
   I = Integer;       { define I as type Integer }
var
   T: I;              { define T as an Integer variable }

   procedure Inner;   { Start of procedure inner scope }
   type
    T = I;            { redefine T as type Integer }
   var
     I: T;            { redefine I as an Integer variable }
   begin
    I := 1;
   end;               { End of procedure inner scope }

begin
   T := 1;
end.                  { End of program outer scope }
```

Local and Global variables

Local variables are variables that exist only within the current scope, for example, within a procedure. Global variables are variables that apply throughout the whole program, generally below where they are declared.

For example:

```
program average5;
var
  x:  integer;

function calc_avg5 : real;
var
  numin, numtotal : integer;
begin
  numtotal:=0;
  for x := 1 to 5 do
  begin
    write('Enter number ', x, ': ');
    readln(numin);
    numtotal:=numtotal+numin;
  end;
  result := numtotal / 5;
end;

var
  avg : real;
begin
  writeln('Enter 5 numbers to get the average');
  avg := calc_avg5;
  writeln('Average is ', avg:4:2);
end.
```

The output from this program is:

```
Enter 5 numbers to get the average
Enter number 1:  2
Enter number 2:  4
Enter number 3:  6
Enter number 4:  8
Enter number 5:  10
Average is 6.00
```

In this example the variable x is considered a *global variable* as it applies to the entire program. The variable x can used in the main code block or within the function as both appear below the declaration of the variable.

The variables numin and numtotal are considered *local variables*, the variables are local to the function calc_avg5. These variables only exist inside the function and can only be called there.

The variable avg, is declared below the function, and cannot be used by the function, but it can be used by any code below the declaration.

Complex Types

Subranges

A subrange type is a range of values of any of the ordinal types such as integer, boolean and char. Subranges are useful when you want to limit the number of values a variable can have. To create a subrange, specify the minimum and maximum values in the range with two periods in between them.

For example:

```
var
   MyOneHundredInts : 1..100;
```

To allow reuse of the subrange, Pascal allows you to declare your own types.

Type - Defining new data types

To declare the subrange from 1 to 100 as a new type and then use it in a variable:

```
type
   TOnetoOneHundred = 1..100;
var
   MyOneHundredInts : TOnetoOneHundred;

begin
   MyOneHundredInts := 76;
```

Because the value 76 is within the range of 1 to 100 the above code works, however if you try to assign a value outside of 1 to 100, such as 101 or 0 or -1, then you will see an Out Of Range error.

Here are some additional type examples for subranges, written as types:

```
type
   TCompassRange = 0..360;
   TValidLetter = 'A'..'F';
   THourlyIncome = 15..300;
   THours = 0..23;
```

Types can be used for many different types of variables, not just subranges.

Arrays

An array is an ordered collection of a data type, with each element of the collection specified by its numeric position within the collection. When the array is created, the elements are not initialized and do not contain useful values, but you can fill them with data and manipulate that data as you need to.

For example, here is a variable declaration for an array of Integer types:

```
var
   MyInts : array [1..10] of Integer;
```

The variable MyInts refers to a list of ten variables of type Integer, each with a number (called its index) from 1 to 10. Each member of an array is referred to as an element.

Each item of an array is referred to by the name of the array, followed by its index enclosed in square brackets [ ]. So the array MyInts contains the ten variables MyInts [1], MyInts [2], MyInts [3], MyInts[4], and so on, up to MyInts [10]. You can use any of these variables wherever you would use a regular Integer variable. Also, the index value doesn't have to be a constant. It can be any expression or variable that yields an integer in the range 1 to 10.

For example:

```
J := 5;
MyInts[J] := 4;
```

The above statements assign the value 4 to variable MyInts[5].

If you want to assign a value of zero to all the MyInts variables in the array, you could use a for loop to do it. Because an index can be a variable, a for loop is easier to use than assigning a value to each item in an array with separate assignment statements. This for loop assigns the value 0 to all ten elements of the MyInts array:

```
for J := 1 to 10 do
   MyInts(J) := 0;
```

Multi-dimensional arrays

The arrays discussed so far are one-dimensional lists. Arrays can have many dimensions. Two-dimensional arrays can be used to hold all the values in a table, for example. You can have as many dimensions are you desire.

This is how you would create a two-dimensional array that can hold all the values in a table that contains 20 columns and 20 rows, using a type declaration:

```
type
   TRealTable = array[1..20, 1..20] of Real;
```

Then you can declare a variable of the TRealTable type:

```
var
   BigTable: TRealTable;
```

To initialise all the values in the table to 0.0, you could use nested for loops:

```
var
   Col, Row: Integer;
begin
for Col := 1 to 20 do
begin
   for Row:= 1 to 20 do
   begin
      BigTable[Col, Row] := 0.0;
   end;
end;
```

These for loops only contain a single statement respectively so we can dispense with the begin and end statements making the code look like this:

```
var
   Col, Row: Integer;
begin
for Col := 1 to 20 do
   for Row:= 1 to 20 do
      BigTable[Col, Row] := 0.0
```

Array as type definition

You can define arrays as types. For example:

```
type
  TMy100Ints = array [1..100] of Integer;
```

You can then declare variables of the array type. For example, this code declares a CheckingAccount to be a variable of type TCheck, which is an array of 100 real numbers.

```
var
 CheckingAccount: TMy100Ints;
```

Simple enumerated values

Enumerated values allow you to give a name for each value in the type, and these values ust be different from values in any other type.

Enumerated values are read from left to right, and have an ordinal value starting at 0.

```
var
   booktype : (paperback, hardback, ebook);
begin
   booktype := ebook;
   if (booktype < ebook) then
```

Once defined, the values included in the enumeration list are now fixed values in the program and cannot be redefined. As these are values, they are not variables and as such they cannot be assigned values. Think of them as constants.

You cannot read values directly into variables of enumerated types, and likewise you cannot output their values directly either.

Generally enumerated values are defined in a type declaration to allow reuse and to use them in function and procedure parameters. You may use an enumerated type when you want a variable to have one of only a few names values, and this is generally done to allow for easy code readability.

Sets

A set is a collection of elements of one type. That one type must be either an integer, boolean, char, enumerated, or subrange type. Sets are useful for checking if a value belongs to a particular set.

Here is a simple example:

```
program vowel_check;
type
  TVowels = set of Char;
var
  Vowels : TVowels;
  ch : char;
begin
  Vowels := ['A','E','I','O','U', 'a','e','i','o','u'];
  write('Enter a Vowel: ');
  readln(ch);
  if (ch in Vowels) then
    writeln('Yes, ', ch, ' is a vowel.')
  else
    writeln('No! ', ch, ' is not a vowel.')
end.
```

The new type TVowels is a set of type Char. Vowels is declared as a variable of type TVowels. The first line of code after the begin reserved word builds the vowel set (puts values into it) and assigns this new set to the Vowels variable. Notice that I included both UPPER case and lower case letters to allow for both in my example.

If the Vowels assignment looked like this:

```
Vowels := [];
```

then the Vowels set would contain no values and would be called an empty set.

The *if* statement uses the *in* operator to see if the value you entered is in the Vowels set.

The expression *ch in Vowels* is a *Boolean* expression that evaluates to either True or False. It tests if the character entered is in the Vowels set.

Records

Records are collections of data that you can refer to as a whole.

For example, you could use a TEmployee record type that is declared like this:

```
type
  TEmployee = record
     LastName  :  string[20];
     FirstName:  string[15];
     YearHired: 1990..2000;
     Salary: Double;
     CompanyPosition: string[20]
  end;
```

Records contain fields that hold data values. Each field has a data type. The fields of a TEmployee type are LastName, FirstName, YearHired, Salary, and CompanyPosition. You can access these fields individually, or you can refer to the record as a whole.

For example, here are the declarations of two record variables:

```
var
 NewEmployee, PromotedEmployee: TEmployee;
```

Your code can refer to the Salary field of a NewEmployee record, like this:

```
NewEmployee.Salary := 43500.00
```

Or your code can manipulate the record as a single entity:

```
PromotedEmployee := NewEmployee;
```

When you refer to a field within a record, you need to type the name of the record, a period (.), and the name of the field:

```
PromotedEmployee.CompanyPosition
```

With statement

If you are going to assign values to fields within a record, you can use the *with* statement. Instead of writing this code:

```
PromotedEmployee.LastName  := 'Jeffries';
PromotedEmployee.FirstName := 'Richard';
PromotedEmployee.YearHired := 1990;
PromotedEmployee.Salary := 100000.00;
PromotedEmployee.CompanyPosition := 'Senior technical
writer';
```

you could assign the values like this:

```
with PromotedEmployee do
  begin
    LastName := 'Jeffries';
    FirstName := 'Richard';
    YearHired := 1990;
    Salary := 100000.00;
    CompanyPosition := 'Senior technical writer';
  end;
```

The purpose of the *with* statement is to make the code shorter and more readable by allowing fields to be referred to without being preceded by the record variable's name.

Text Files

You can use the read and write statements to read from and write to text files similarly to the keyboard and screen.

To use a textfile in your program you will need to declare a variable of type textfile, and assign it to a filename. It is also important to remember to close the file after you are finished writing to it.

Writing to a text file

```
program writefile;
var
   outfile : textfile;
begin
   assignfile(outfile, 'text.txt');
   rewrite(outfile);
   writeln(outfile,'Sample text');
   close(outfile);
end.
```

Outfile is defined as type *textfile*, which is a reserved word in Pascal. The statement *assignfile* assigns the textfile variable to an actual file, in this case a file called text.txt in the same directory as the program.

The *rewrite* command opens the file for writing (not reading) and clears the contents if the file already exists. This deletes any existing file called text.txt so this command should be used with care. You can test if a file already exists with the same name by using the function *fileexists*, which returns a Boolean value, e.g. true if a file with that name already exists.

The writeln command includes as the first parameter the textfile to write to. If this is omitted it will simply write to the screen.

The close command closes the specified textfile and ensures all data is written to the file.

Once the program is finished, a file called text.txt will exist in the same directory as the program and will contain one line of text.

Reading from a text file

```
program readfile;
var
   infile : textfile;
   str : string;
begin
   assignfile(infile, 'text.txt');
   reset(infile);
   readln(infile, str);
   close(infile);
   writeln(str);
end.
```

Infile is defined as type *textfile* and the statement *assignfile* assigns the textfile variable to an actual file, in this case a file called text.txt in the same directory as the program.

The *reset* command opens the file for reading (not writing) and positions the cursor at the start of the file.

The readln command includes as the first parameter the textfile to read from. If this is omitted it will simply read from the keyboard.

The close command closes the specified textfile.

This program reads the first line of text from the file and displays it on the screen.

Units

A unit is a separate Pascal file containing collection of constants, data types, variables, and procedures and functions that can be shared by several applications allowing code reuse, or used by a single application only. Pascal comes with a large number of predefined units you use to construct your program, and you can also create your own.

An example of a predefined unit is the *Math* unit which contains a large number of mathematical functions you can call.

The basic structure of a unit is generally as follows:

```
unit <identifier>;

interface

uses <list of units>;        { optional }

{ public declarations }
implementation

uses <list of units>;        { optional }

{ private declarations }

{ implementation of procedures and functions }

initialization          { optional }

{ optional initialization code}

end;
```

The unit header starts with the reserved word *unit*, followed by the unit's name (an identifier). The next item in a unit is the reserved word *interface*, which indicates the beginning of the interface part of the unit – the part visible to other units or applications that use this unit. This section will contain prototypes that can be called from outside the unit.

A program or other unit can use the declarations in other units by specifying those units in a *uses* clause. The uses clause can appear in two places, in the interface section and in the implementation section:

It can appear after the reserved word *interface*.

Any code in the current unit can use the declarations declared in the interface parts of the units specified in the uses clause.

For example, suppose you are writing code in unit A, and you want to call a procedure declared in the interface part of unit B. Once you add the name of unit B to the uses clause in the interface part of unit A, any code in unit A can call the procedure declared in unit B.

If unit B is in the uses clause in the interface part of unit A, unit A cannot be in the uses clause in the interface part of unit B. This creates a circular unit reference, and when you attempt to compile, Pascal generates an error message.

It can appear after the reserved word *implementation*.

Only declarations in the current unit can use the declarations in the interface parts of the units specified here. Any other units that use the current unit won't be able to use the units listed in this uses clause.

For example, if unit C is in a uses clause in the implementation part of unit B, and unit B is in a uses clause of unit A, unit A can use only the declarations in the interface parts of unit B. Unit A can't access the declarations in unit C, unless unit C is in a uses clause of unit A.

If unit B is in the uses clause in the implementation part of unit A, unit A can be in the uses clause in the implementation part of unit B. While circular unit references are not allowed in the interface part, they are fine in the implementation part.

Interface part

The interface part of a unit begins with the reserved word *interface*, which appears after the unit header and ends at the reserved word *implementation*. The interface determines what is "visible" (accessible) to any application or other unit using this unit.

The procedures and functions visible to any unit or application using the unit are declared in the interface part. Their actual code is found in the implementation part. You don't need to use forward declarations, and forwards are not allowed in the interface part.

An optional uses clause can appear in the interface and must immediately follow the *interface* reserved word.

Implementation part

The implementation part of a unit begins with the reserved word *implementation*. Everything declared in the interface part is accessible to the code in the implementation part.

The implementation can have additional declarations of its own, although these declarations aren't accessible to any other application or unit. These declarations are used by the procedures and functions declared in this unit.

An optional uses clause can appear in the implementation part and follows the *implementation* reserved word.

The bodies of the routines declared in the interface part must appear in the implementation part. The procedure or function header that appears in the implementation part can be identical to the declaration that appears in the interface part, or it can be in the short form.

Procedure and Function short form names

To use the short form names, enter the procedure or function reserved word and follow it with the routine's name. You can omit any list of parameters, and, if the routine is a function, the return type.

For example, you declare this function in the interface part:

```
Interface

  function CalculateInterest(Principal, InterestRate:Double):
Double;
```

When you write the body of the function in the implementation part, you can choose to write the function like this:

```
Implementation

  function CalculateInterest;
  begin
    Result := Principal * InterestRate;
  end;
```

Note that the parameter and the return type have been omitted.

If you declare any routines in the implementation part (not in the interface part), you must use the long form of the procedure or function header.

Initialization part

If you want to initialize any data the unit uses or makes available through the interface part to the application or unit using it, you can add an *initialization* part to the unit. Above the final *end* reserved word at the bottom of the unit, add the reserved word *initialization*. Between the initialization and end reserved words, you write the code that initializes the data.

For example:

```
Implementation

  { Functions and Procedures }

Initialization

  { Your initialization code goes here }

end.
```

When an application uses a unit, the code within the unit's initialization part is called before the any other application code runs. If the application uses more than one unit, each unit's initialization part is called before the rest of the application runs.

Finalization part

If your unit needs to perform any cleanup when the application terminates, such as freeing any resources allocated in the initialization part, you can add a finalization part to your unit. The finalization part comes after the initialization part, but before the final end.

For example:

```
Initialization

   { Your initialization code goes here }

finalization

   { Your finalization code goes here }

end.
```

When an application terminates, it executes the finalization sections of its units in the opposite order it initialized them.

Exercise: Create a Unit that contains a Procedure, and call that procedure from your main program.

www.ingramcontent.com/pod-product-compliance
Lightning Source LLC
LaVergne TN
LVHW051749050326
832903LV00029B/2807